Grolier
Album
Series

THE FUR TRADE IN CANADA

Keith Wilson

Grolier Limited
TORONTO

Copyright © 1983 by Grolier Limited. All rights reserved.

CANADIAN CATALOGUING IN PUBLICATION DATA

Wilson, Keith, 1929-
  The fur trade in Canada

(Grolier album series)
ISBN 0-7172-1824-4

1. Fur trade—Canada—History. 2. Hudson's Bay
Company—History. I. Title. II. Series.

FC3207.W55   971   C83-098348-1
F1060.W55

Printed and Bound in Canada

Introduction

Canada was molded by the Ice Age and developed by the fur trade. When the glaciers of the Ice Age melted, they left behind a land dotted with lakes and streams, an ideal home for fur-bearing animals. Then the first human inhabitants, the ancestors of the Indians, arrived from Asia and gradually spread over the continent. They were followed about 5000 years ago by the ancestors of the Inuit, but Europeans remained ignorant of the North American continent until John Cabot's voyage to Newfoundland in 1497. Although Cabot's reports of seas teeming with fish attracted European fishermen, no further attempts at discovery took place until 1534 when Jacques Cartier explored the Gulf of St. Lawrence. At the Gaspé Peninsula he met some Indians who willingly bartered even the furs they were wearing. Thus began the fur trade in Canada.

The new trade developed slowly, with the traders exchanging knives and tools for animal pelts. Specially prized were beaver pelts for use in the manufacture of felt hats. Enterprising Frenchmen began to organize trading companies, one of which sent Champlain to begin the settlement of Canada. In 1608 he established a permanent base at Quebec, and from this grew the colony of New France.

The fledgling colony attracted adventurers, farmers and priests, but it depended for its existence on the profits of the fur trade. These in turn depended on regular supplies from the Indians in the interior. Warfare between rival tribes frequently interrupted fur shipments and soon involved the French in Indian quarrels. Moreover, the English, traditional enemies of the French, were also attracted by the profits to be made.

Eventually England claimed the vast area that drained into Hudson Bay and, in 1670, granted it to the newly formed Hudson's Bay Company. The Company began building trading posts along the shores of the Bay, and there followed a period of intense English-French rivalry and frequent bloodshed. In 1713 France gave up her claims to the Hudson Bay region, but French traders pushed west into the prairies to cut off the inland fur trade from their English rivals. The English were saved from further French competition only by Britain's conquest of New France in 1759-60.

(THE WELLINGTON.)
(1812)

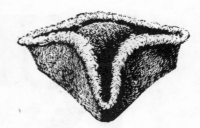

"CONTINENTAL"
COCKED HAT.
(1776)

CLERICAL.
(Eighteenth Century)

The soft woolly underfur of the beaver was ideal for making a durable felt that could be shaped into different styles of hat. By the early seventeenth century, beaver hats had become so popular in Europe that the European beaver was fast nearing extinction. Demand continued to grow, spurring efforts to establish permanent trading posts in Canada.

Furs were greatly prized in the sixteenth century and were often worn as a sign of wealth or noble birth. This portrait of a young and rather bored Italian nobleman was painted sometime between 1530 and 1540, and it clearly shows the rich fur trimming of his cloak. Furs were also used for lining clothes, particularly in the colder countries of northern Europe.

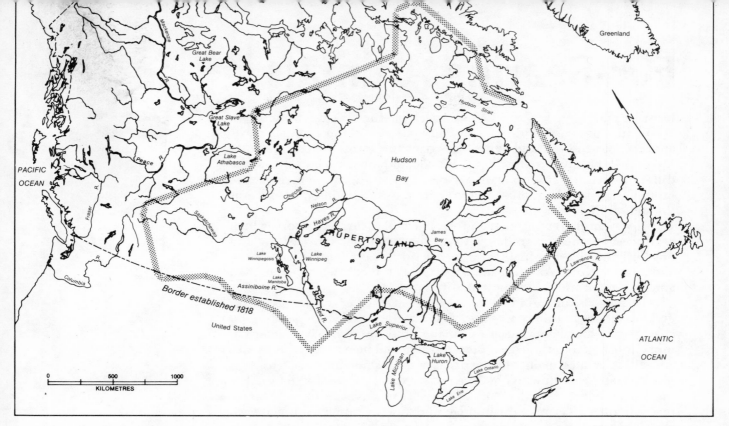

With its cold climate and its thousands of lakes and connecting streams, Canada is an ideal home for fur-bearing animals. The shaded area on this map outlines the Hudson Bay drainage basin, that is, the territory granted to the Hudson's Bay Company and known as Rupert's Land.

The men of the Hudson's Bay Company were now seemingly secure on the shores of Hudson Bay, but they soon had to face renewed opposition. Fur traders from the East and from the American colonies took over the abandoned French posts. They later formed the North West Company and penetrated to the Pacific coast and to the rich fur country of the Athabasca. It was on the long and arduous supply routes of the North West Company that the voyageurs built their colourful reputations.

In 1812 the beginning of agricultural settlement at Red River, an area which lay across the main supply route of the Nor'Westers, completely changed the picture. Rivalry between the two companies became more serious and more violent. Trading was disrupted, profits declined and both companies suffered. The only sensible answer was amalgamation, and the two rivals formally united in 1821 under the name of the Hudson's Bay Company.

The new company was reorganized by the ruthlessly efficient Sir George Simpson, and under his leadership it enjoyed nearly forty profitable years. But by the 1860s times were changing, and in 1869 the Company transferred its lands to the new Canadian nation. Though still rich and influential, the historic Hudson's Bay Company was now but a trading company.

Since that time the fur trade has lost some of its importance as Canada has become an agricultural and industrial nation, but furs still represent a significant part of the nation's economy and Canada is still among the foremost fur-producing countries of the world.

The fur trade played a unique role in Canada's story and, for better or worse, has left its mark indelibly on the nation's history.

FOR DISCOVERY

1. What were furs used for in the Middle Ages?
2. For centuries kings, lords, judges and scholars wore furs, and furs are still worn in many countries on ceremonial occasions. Can you name any ceremony in Canada where furs are still worn?
3. What are the main uses of furs today?

Fur-Bearing Animals

Most animals have fur, so when we speak of "fur-bearing" animals we are including a very wide range of animals—from the aquatic beaver and otter to the fox and lynx that roam the forests; from the little squirrel and ermine to the mighty buffalo and moose. The value of the different furs depends on many factors. To the English nobleman, the buffalo was of little interest and no value; to the Plains Indian it was the staff of life.

It was an increasing demand for particular furs in Europe which really began the fur trade in Canada. Supplies from eastern and northern Europe gradually declined, and traders had to look more and more to North America and particularly Canada, where the terrain and climate produced the best quality furs.

Because its fur was ideal for making felt, the beaver was always in great demand, but there was also a continuing market, depending on changing fashions and prices, for many other furs: fox, lynx, marten, mink, muskrat, otter, raccoon, seal and skunk. The market for furs was, and still is, created mainly by the needs of the fashion industry. Fashions often change very quickly, but the more expensive and higher quality the fur, the more desirable and fashionable it often is. Current market prices in turn determine the number and kind of animals trapped each year for their furs.

Beaver

The beaver is now found in great numbers only in North America. One of the largest rodents, it often reaches 1.3 metres in length and can weigh nearly thirty kilograms. It is a thickset animal with prominent and very sharp incisor teeth, short front paws and webbed hind feet. Its tail is scaly and paddle-shaped. The fur consists of a thick woolly undercoat covered by a layer of shiny guard hairs.

Beavers are agile in water but clumsy on land. For safety, therefore, they always live where there are trees and water. With their sharp teeth they cut down trees to form the basis of dams which, with the addition of sticks, mud and debris, often reach great size. Once the dam has raised the water level and formed a pond, the beavers build their house, or lodge, on an island of sticks and mud.

Each spring the female beaver gives birth to a litter of three or four kits. These youngsters usually stay with their parents for two years and then seek their own mates and build their own homes.

Marten

Sometimes known as Canadian sable, the marten is a member of the weasel family and inhabits forested areas. It lives mainly in the trees but also hunts on the ground. It is carnivorous and sufficiently agile to catch squirrels, which are its favourite food. The fur varies in colour from dark brown to pale yellow. Litters, usually of two or three babies, are born in the spring. While valuable for its fur, the marten's flesh, according to one trader, had a "rank, disagreeable taste; and is, therefore, seldom eaten."

Buffalo

The American bison, commonly called the buffalo, at one time roamed the prairies in enormous herds. Their total numbers probably reached 60 million.

Buffalo are usually dark brown in colour, with the head and shoulders almost black. The male stands over two metres high and weighs nearly a thousand kilograms; the females are about half this size.

The buffalo provided just about all the needs of the Plains Indians: food, clothing, tipi coverings, utensils and even fuel. Traders in the early 1800s listed buffalo furs among the ten most valuable. They were usually used for robes and rugs.

Mink

Most mink now come from ranches where they are bred and raised in captivity, but wild mink were long important in the fur trade.

The mink, a member of the weasel family, has short legs, a slender body about half a metre long, and weighs about one kilogram. On land the mink moves in a series of bounds, but in water it is as much at home as the otter. It is usually found in wooded areas near water where it lives in tree trunks or other sheltered spots. It eats birds, fish and small animals. Fur quality and colour vary, but the best furs, which are found in the far northwest, are a soft brownish colour.

Harp seal

All seals are marine animals which come ashore only to breed.
For purposes of the fur trade, there are two basic types of
seal: the fur seal with a dense covering of underfur, and the hair
seal with almost no underfur. Of most value to Canadians is
the harp seal, which is a species of hair seal.

The harp seal migrates, spending the months of the
Arctic summer in northern feeding grounds near Baffin Island
and then moving south with the ice floes to its breeding
grounds off the Newfoundland coast and in the Gulf of St.
Lawrence. Here the pups are born in the spring. At birth
they have a covering of white downy fur which they begin to shed
after ten days and which is highly prized for collars and
trimming.

Otter

The otter is a member of the weasel family. Typically
weighing about ten kilograms, it has a long body, webbed feet and
a long, broad tail. It lives near lakes and streams and is an
expert swimmer and diver. It feeds mainly on fish, frogs and
other small animals. The underfur of the otter is dense and
dark bluish-brown in colour.

The otter is a playful animal and enjoys sliding down
river banks and juggling pebbles on its nose. But it will defend
itself if pursued and has been known to attack dogs and even
men. One unusual fact about the otter: European otters like to
whistle but North American otters grunt and rumble. They
can all chuckle and chirp, and when angry they can all scream.

The sea otter, a close relative, was once common along
the Pacific coast but was over-hunted and is now very rare.

Muskrat

The musquash or muskrat is much smaller than the beaver but is very similar in its habits. It lives in swamps or near slow-running streams where it builds a conical home of roots and twigs plastered with mud. It feeds mainly on roots and plants but, unlike the beaver, also eats fish. The muskrat, so called because it gives off a musk scent, breeds very quickly and has several litters a year. Even the young start breeding after a few months.

Fox

The typical fox is a slender animal with large ears, a pointed snout and a long bushy tail. It eats just about anything, including fowl and small animals. It lives in burrows, prowls largely at night and has a well-earned reputation for being sly and cunning. About the fox's fur, Daniel Harmon, a Nor'Wester for nearly twenty years, noted in 1816: "The most common are of a yellowish red, some are of a beautiful silver grey, and some in the more northern latitudes, are almost black. The last, are by far the most valuable."

Lynx

The lynx, a member of the cat family has large paws which act somewhat like snowshoes and help it to cross deep snow. Daniel Harmon wrote in his journal:

The cat or lynx, in its shape and nature resembles the domestic cat; but it is much larger, it has long legs, and a long body; but a very short tail. Its hair is exceedingly fine, considerably long, and of a lively and beautiful, silver grey colour. When full grown, the cat will weigh thirty-five or forty pounds [16-18 kg]; and when fat they are excellent food. They generally live on mice, the dead fish which they find along the rivers and lakes, and partridges and hares. . . . In some years, these animals are very numerous; and, frequently, the following year, very few can be found.

FOR DISCOVERY

1. Why are the best quality furs often found in areas with extremely cold winters?
2. What is meant by "the fur industry"?
3. Find pictures of three fur-bearing animals not mentioned here. Find out where they live, what they eat and what their fur is used for.
4. Visit your nearest zoo for a look at some of the fur-bearing animals.

Hunting and Trapping

The Indians were hunting and trapping wild animals for both meat and fur before the arrival of the Europeans. Their methods, of course, varied according to the type of animal and the weapons they had available.

For some smaller animals the usual trap was a deadfall: an animal, lured by bait, would trigger a device which dropped a log across its neck, killing it instantly. The beaver was a more certain victim, for the hunter could quite easily find and break open the beaver lodges during the winter. Other common methods were to break the dams and drain the ponds where the beaver could hide, or even to drop dust down the air vents and force the beavers out into underwater nets.

For killing larger animals such as deer or moose, the Indians had to depend on spears and bows and arrows; but they thought up some clever ways to make their hunting easier. For instance, they sometimes stampeded the buffalo into enclosures, known as pounds, or over a cliff. Later, the two annual buffalo hunts became large and well-planned expeditions organized by the Métis.

Guns made it much easier to kill many animals, but as a means of getting pelts for the fur trade, they had drawbacks. There was always a risk of damaging the fur and where feasible, trappers used other methods. In some remote areas they used poisoned bait or devised snares made from wire or saplings.

Before Indian hunters had guns, their big problem was to get close enough to the buffalo to use their spears or arrows. One answer was to stampede them into an enclosure where the nearsighted animals could easily be slaughtered.

Indians breaking into a beaver lodge. This method, of course, could only be used in the winter, when the ice was strong, but that was when beaver fur was at its best.

C.W. JEFFERYS

The two annual Métis buffalo hunts were large, well-organized expeditions. The June hunt in 1840, for example, involved 1210 carts and 1630 men, women and children. The hunts took place under definite rules, the breaking of which was severely punished. Can you imagine what some of these rules might have been and why they were so important?

The big advance in trapping was the introduction about 1797 of the iron trap. This, later improved and made of steel, soon became the most common method of trapping fur-bearing animals. The main problem with steel traps is that they are cruel. The animal is not killed outright unless the trap is set underwater and it drowns. Usually it is held by the leg and suffers great pain as it struggles to break free. Although these traps are still widely used, the most commonly recommended trap today is the Conibear, named after its Canadian inventor, which kills trapped animals instantly.

Almost as important as the trap are the lures—the scents or baits used to entice the animal into it. The recommended lures vary greatly: mink musk mixed with honey will attract most animals. Cheap perfume from a store will attract ermine, while carrots or orange peel are excellent lures for muskrat.

Experienced trappers soon learn not to underestimate their prey. Some animals are very cunning and often learn to outwit the inexperienced trapper.

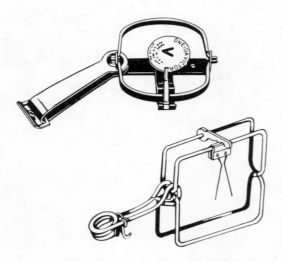

The iron or steel leg trap consists of two metal jaws which are hinged so that they lie flat when the trap is set. In the centre is a pan with a trigger attached. When the animal steps on the pan, it sets off the trigger. The jaws snap together and lock around the animal's leg. The traps are usually chained to a stake or a tree so that the animal cannot escape by dragging them away.

More humane than the leg trap, the Conibear trap is designed to catch smaller animals around the neck or chest. It closes with such force that the animal is usually killed instantly.

It was often wise to go trapping with a partner:

Sickness rarely overtakes a trapper; the outdoor life they practice is conducing to good health.. but there is always the risk of accident, accident in many ways. The guns, the axe, the canoe breaking through the ice, or even getting caught in one of his own traps; in fact by the last mentioned source of danger I have known two men to lose their lives in a most horrible way of torture and agony, and these men were not novices at the business; one was . . . born and brought up to trapping, and the other was an old Nova Scotian who had trapped and hunted for forty years.

The life of the trapper could be exciting but it also had its hardships:

The long laborious march, loaded with a heavy pack, and covered with a quantity of thick clothing, through snow and woods beset with fallen timber and underbrush, is fatiguing enough. Provisions usually fall short, and the trapper subsists, in a great measure, on the animals captured to obtain the fur. . . . The only change in the fatiguing monotony is the work of making traps, or the rest in camp at night.

Trappers always tried to make sure of their food supplies by building caches:

If a party is to return on the outgoing trail ... it is very easy to cache [food] for the home journey with a certainty of finding it "after many days," that is, if properly secured. If in the depth of winter, and there is a likelihood of wolves or wolverines coming that way, a good and safe way is to cut a hole in the ice some distance from the shore on some big lake, cutting almost through to the water. In this trench put what is required to be left behind, filling up with the chopped ice, tramp this well down, then pour several kettles of water on top. This freezes at once, making it as difficult to gnaw or scratch into as would be the side of an ironclad. I have come on such a cache after an absence of three weeks to find the droppings of wolves and foxes about, but the contents untouched. One could not help smiling on seeing these signs, imagining the profound thinking the animals must have exerted in trying to figure out a plan to reach the toothsome stuff under that hard, glazed surface.

Resource officials release beaver to repopulate wilderness areas.

Conservation

If trappers killed as many animals as they wished, two things might happen; so few would be left to breed that the animals would decrease or even become extinct; too many furs would go to auction and prices would go down. It makes sense, then, to limit the number of animals killed each year. Provincial governments do this by issuing trapping licences and by limiting the time each year when different types of animals may be killed.

William Cormack, who travelled across Newfoundland in 1822, noted that the Indians who hunted beaver also practised conservation:

On account of the value of the skin, beavers are the chief object of the chase with the Indians. These people, having made themselves acquainted with the different spots throughout the Island where these animals abound most, hunt over these places alternately and periodically, allowing the beavers three years to regenerate.

FOR DISCOVERY

1. What is meant by conservation? Why is it important to the fur trade?
2. Do you think that most animals are intelligent?
3. What were some of the problems faced by trappers in 1800? Are today's problems any different?
4. Using pieces of wood and string, design and build a simple deadfall trap.
5. The success of a hunter or trapper often depends on his knowledge of the animal's habits and weaknesses. Read about three animals and list any weakness that makes it easier to kill them.
6. Have a class debate on the motion ... "That trapping is cruel and should be banned."

Fur Trade Companies

By 1600 there was a great demand in Europe for all furs, but especially beaver. Enterprising French merchants began to organize companies and to build permanent trading posts in New France. The French kings supported these companies by granting them monopolies, that is the sole right to trade in certain areas. In return, the companies agreed to help build up the colony. The most famous of these companies was the Company of New France, popularly known as the Company of One Hundred Associates, which held the fur trade monopoly for all of New France from 1627 to 1663.

English competition became a serious threat to the French fur trade in 1670 when the Hudson's Bay Company was created. The company's charter gave it not only a trading monopoly but also outright ownership of all the lands draining into Hudson Bay.

Within a few years the Company had established a number of posts along the shores of the Bay. The French tried to compete and attacked the English posts, but the British had the stronger navy and the more dependable supply route. In 1713 the French withdrew their claims to this area and turned all their attention to strengthening their hold on the inland waterways. Led by such men as La Vérendrye, they established posts as far west as Lake Winnipegosis.

Indispensable to the fur trading companies of New France were the *coureurs de bois*, the young men who ranged the forests in search of furs. Denis Riverin, a citizen of New France, wrote this account of them in 1705:

Coureurs de bois *are Frenchmen who were either born in Canada or who came to settle there. They are always young men in the prime of life, for old age cannot endure the hardships of this occupation. . . .*

Since all of Canada is a vast and trackless forest, it is impossible for them to travel by land: they travel by lake and river in canoes ordinarily occupied by three men. . . .

[They] embark at Quebec or Montreal to go three hundred, four hundred, and sometimes five hundred lieues [2000 km] to search for beaver among Indians whom they have frequently never seen. Their entire provisions consist of a little biscuit, peas, corn, and a few small casks of brandy. They carry as little as possible in order to make room for a few bundles of merchandise and are soon obliged to live from hunting and fishing. . . . If fish and game are scarce, as frequently happens, they are obliged to eat a sort of moss, which they call tripe, *that grows on rocks. With it they make a broth that is black and loathsome but which they would rather eat than die of starvation. If they have nothing to eat on their return journey or on their travels from one tribe to another they will resort to their moccasins or to a glue they make from the skins they have bartered.*

. . . They endure the jeers, the scorn, and sometimes the blows of the Indians, who are constantly amazed by . . . Frenchmen who come from so far away at the cost of great hardship and expense to pick up dirty, stinking beaver pelts which they have worn and have discarded.

Ironically, it was two French adventurers, Pierre Esprit Radisson and Médard Chouart, sieur des Groseilliers, who brought the potential wealth of the Hudson Bay region to the attention of the English. Mother Marie de l'Incarnation writes of Groseilliers' success at the English court:

Some time ago a Frenchman . . ., named des Groseilliers, married in this country and, not making a great fortune, he took a fancy to go to New England to try to make a better one. . . . He gave the English reason to hope he might find the passage through the Sea of the North [Hudson Bay]. In hope of this, they equipped him to go to England, where he was given a vessel with men and all items necessary for navigation and exploration. . . . Instead of taking the route others had taken and found vain, he sailed against the wind and searched so successfully that he found the great Bay of the North. There he loaded . . . his ship (or his ships) with pelts worth immense sums. He returned to England, where the King gave him a reward of twenty thousand écus and made him a Knight of the Garter, which is said to be a very honourable rank. He took possession of this great country for the King of England and, with respect to himself, he became rich in a very little time.

Before being abandoned, the *Pélican*, commanded by Pierre Lemoyne d'Iberville, had single-handedly sunk one British ship, captured a second and driven off a third. The French went on to take York Fort, but it was returned to the British by a peace treaty signed later that year.

First page of the Hudson's Bay Company Charter

Although the French threat to the Hudson's Bay Company came to an end in 1763, British merchants in Montreal and ambitious traders from New England soon took over the forts and supply system the French had built. They began to form small, loosely organized companies, and one large company eventually emerged: the North West Company. With the operations of the Nor'Westers stretching right across Rupert's Land, which belonged by charter to the Hudson's Bay Company, there was bound to be trouble. When Lord Selkirk established an agricultural settlement at Red River, the Nor'Westers' supply route was seriously threatened. Bloodshed occurred at Seven Oaks in 1816, violence continued and trade suffered. Finally, under pressure from the British government, the two companies merged in 1821 under the name of the older company. But now, as in the former North West Company, the actual traders were to share in the profits.

The new company enjoyed forty good years. But by the 1860s settlements at Red River and at Victoria were thriving and becoming resentful of Company rule. The trade monopoly could no longer be enforced. The end was inevitable, and in 1869 the Company transferred its lands to the new Dominion of Canada.

North West Company partners meet at Fort William

Notice what the Hudson's Bay Company promised to pay a labourer in return for his work. How could you decide whether this man was to be well paid?

MEMORANDUM of an Agreement entered into the First of June, 1812, by and between the Hudson's Bay Company, of the one Part and *Joseph Kenny* of the other Part,

WITNESSETH That the said *Joseph Kenny* for the considerations hereinafter mentioned, doth covenant, promise and agree to serve honestly and faithfully the said Hudson's Bay Company, in British North America, as a *labourer* for all lawful purposes in which the said Company may chuse to employ him for the full space and term of Three Years, to commence from the First of June, 1812, Inst. and to be subservient to the orders and directions of all such Persons as shall be placed over him by said Company; and said Company doth promise, covenant and agree, to find the said *Joseph Kenny* in a suitable free passage out, and to furnish good and wholesome Provisions and Lodgings, and all other necessaries, Clothing excepted, for the full space and term of Three Years, to commence from the First of June, Instant, and to pay the sum of *Twenty Twenty* British, sterling, as Yearly Wages, for all and every year, for said Three Years, and at the expiration of said Three Years, to provide the said *Joseph Kenny* with a Free Passage home in their Ships, should the said *Joseph Kenny* chose to

When fur trade rivalry was still intense, the Nor'Westers prepared for violence. One man confessed in 1821:

I, Julien Tavurnur dit St. Picqué . . . do voluntarily declare that . . . in the course of the Summer of 1812 I came to the N. W. Coys. establishment at Fort William . . . and while there that A. N. McLeod, & George Keith, both Partners of the N. W. Coy spoke to me and said, that as I was a stout powerful man, my services would be required as a Bully in Athabasca to fight with and beat the servants of the H. B. Coy. . . . and that if I made myself active and conspicuous in that way, I should be handsomely rewarded.

The leading Nor'Westers were arrogant and loved to show off their wealth. A visitor to Montreal commented:

It was no uncommon thing for a dashing North Wester to parade the streets of the city with his horse shod with silver shoes, nor to be seen throwing handfulls of small coins among the children of the habitants on his visits through the country.

The Hudson's Bay Company was constantly recruiting new employees, usually in Scotland. This advertisement appeared in the *Inverness Journal* on April 19, 1811:

A few young, active, stout men for the service of the Hudson's Bay Company at their factories and settlements in America. The wages given from the date of embarkation, is twenty pounds a year inclusive of sufficient allowance of good wholesome food. . . . Five pounds, if required, will be advanced of the wages at shipping.

The Council of the Northern Department of the Hudson's Bay Company meeting at Norway House, June 21, 1836.

Simon McTavish, one of the founders of the North West Company

FOR DISCOVERY

1. A monopoly gives exclusive control and rights to an individual or group, thereby denying any competition. The Hudson's Bay Company was given a monopoly to a certain area for fur-trading rights. What are the main advantages and disadvantages of a monopoly? Do we have any monopolies today?
2. By the charter of 1670 Charles II of England granted about half of modern Canada to the Hudson's Bay Company. Did he have the right to do so?
3. Why do you think so many young men in Scotland were eager to join the Hudson's Bay Company?
4. What were the main strengths and weaknesses of the Hudson's Bay and the North West companies?
5. What were the advantages of merging the two companies in 1821?

Why do you think Governor Simpson took a bagpiper with him on his inspection tours?

Fur Forts

When fur traders first penetrated into unknown country, their immediate thought was for their own safety and the protection of their supplies. They were quick to build shelters, using the material closest at hand. Thus the forts of the fur trade usually consisted of a palisade of wooden stakes surrounding an inner yard with one or two meagre huts. They stood on the bank of a river or the shore of a lake, while behind them stretched the boundless forests.

In the days of New France, when the threat of Indian attacks was very real, the fur traders paid great attention to defences. This practice continued as their forts gradually extended westward to Lake Superior and beyond. Similarly, the early forts of the Hudson's Bay Company were well prepared to resist any but the most determined attack. Once the Anglo-French rivalry had ended, however, only a few of the major forts were well defended.

Eventually the forts of the fur trade came to vary considerably in size and importance. Strung out along remote waterways from Labrador to the Pacific coast were hundreds of small posts where goods were exchanged for furs. These were sent to the larger forts every spring as soon as the ice was off the waterways.

Most activity occurred at these larger forts, or factories, where a year's supply of food and provisions was sorted. The two most important ones were the Hudson's Bay Company's York Factory on Hudson Bay and the North West Company's Fort William on Lake Superior. There were several other large fur forts, including Upper and Lower Fort Garry in present-day Manitoba and Fort St. James in the northern interior of British Columbia. Conditions at these forts could be fairly comfortable.

By the middle of the nineteenth century many of the small, isolated posts still remained, as they do today, but settlements had grown up around Fort William, Fort Garry and Fort Victoria. There, retired Hudson's Bay Company officers and employees joined farmers and merchants to form thriving communities. This trend continued as settlement spread across the prairies and towns sprang up around the trading posts at Brandon House and Fort Edmonton; it ended with the opening of overland routes and the building of railways.

The Quebec habitation, built by Champlain in 1608

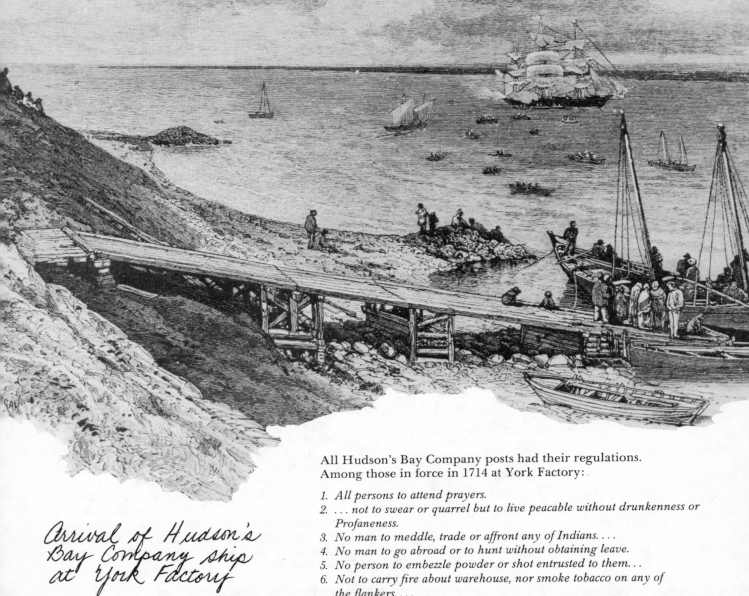

Arrival of Hudson's Bay Company ship at York Factory

All Hudson's Bay Company posts had their regulations. Among those in force in 1714 at York Factory:

1. *All persons to attend prayers.*
2. *... not to swear or quarrel but to live peacable without drunkenness or Profaneness.*
3. *No man to meddle, trade or affront any of Indians....*
4. *No man to go abroad or to hunt without obtaining leave.*
5. *No person to embezzle powder or shot entrusted to them...*
6. *Not to carry fire about warehouse, nor smoke tobacco on any of the flankers....*
7. *No man to go off duty until he sees the next one up....*
8. *To live lovingly and do things with cheerfulness.*

Fort Chipewyan on Lake Athabasca was the North West Company's most important northern post.

18

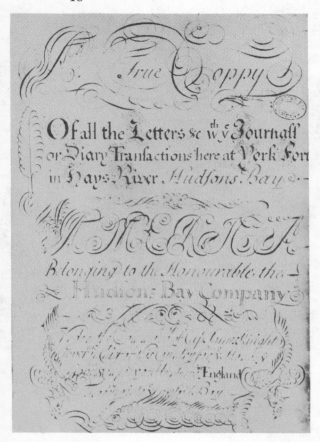

Title page of York Fort Journal, 1714-15

To young men who enjoyed outdoor life, the work of a Company clerk could be tedious. At least it was for Robert Ballantyne:

Soon after my arrival, I underwent the operation which my horse had undergone before me, viz. that of being broken in; the only difference being, that he was broken in to the saddle and I to the desk. It is needless to describe the agonies I endured while sitting, hour after hour, on a long-legged stool ... while the twittering of birds, barking of dogs, lowing of cows, and neighing of horses, seemed now to invite me to join them in the woods; and anon ... their voices seemed to change to hoarse derisive laughter, as if they thought that the little mis-shapen frogs croaking and whistling in the marshes were freer far than their proud masters.

For many years Fort William was the North West Company's most important depot. Its buildings included a large house for the partner in charge, a council house, a doctor's residence, several buildings to accomodate workmen and traders from the interior, a forge and various other work-shops, extensive stores for trading goods and furs, and even a jail. Outside the walls were a shipyard, where the company's vessels were built and repaired, and a farm, where grain and vegetables were grown and animals raised for domestic use.

*Carpenter's shop
at Fort William*

*Two types
of fur
press*

Sheep grazing among the buildings at Fort William. Why did the larger forts often have farms? Some smaller posts had farms; others did not. How do you account for this?

Henry Moberly comments on the record
kept at Hudson's Bay Company posts in the 1850s:

*Each post had also to keep a diary of the weather,
work done, annual departures, births, deaths,
marriages and all other events.*

*Some of these records were rather amusing. I
noticed one which set out that on a certain day "the
wind was northwest; a band of Indians camped round;
all hands chopping cordwood," and that "Mrs.
Bellerose was delivered of a fine girl." And for the next
thirteen days the dates were duly written and the
words perfunctorily added, "All the same as yesterday."
So it would appear ... that poor Mrs. Bellerose
had become the mother of fourteen children in as
many days.*

*Governor Simpson
arriving at Ft. St. James
in the northern interior
of British Columbia*

Robert Ballantyne describes Bachelor's Hall, York Factory,
in 1843:

*The house was only one storey high, and the greater part of the
interior formed a large hall, from which several doors led into the sleep-
ing apartment of the clerks. The whole was built of wood; and few
houses could be found wherein so little attention was paid to ornament or
luxury. The walls were originally painted white; but this, from long
exposure to the influence of a large smoky stove, had changed to a dirty
yellow. No carpet covered the floor. ... The only furniture that
graced the room consisted of two small kitchen tables without table-cloths,
five whole wooden chairs, and a broken one; which latter, being light
and handy, was occasionally used as a missile by the young men when
they happened to quarrel.*

Robert Ballantyne describes how the
people at York Factory coped
with the cold winters:

*To resist this intense cold, the inhabitants
dress, not in furs, as is generally
supposed, but in coats and trousers
made of smoked deerskins: the only piece
of fur in their costume being the
cap. The houses are built of wood, with
double windows and doors. They
are heated by large iron stoves, fed with
wood; yet so intense is the cold, that
I have seen the stove in places red-hot,
and a basin of water in the room
frozen solid.*

York Factory

Dr. Cheadle, who crossed Canada in the early 1860s, described Fort Edmonton:

The establishment at Edmonton is the most important one in the Saskatchewan district. . . . It boasts of a windmill, a blacksmith's forge, and carpenter's shop. The boats required for the annual voyage to York Factory in Hudson's Bay are built and mended here; carts, sleighs, and harness made, and all appliances required for the Company's traffic between the different posts.

Upper Fort Garry, 1845

William Francis Butler, a British officer who travelled through the Northwest in 1872, recalls the welcome sight of a Hudson's Bay Company post after a long journey:

Wild, desolate and remote are these isolated trading spots, yet it is difficult to describe the feelings with which one beholds them across some ice-bound lake, or silent river as the dog trains wind slowly amidst the snow. Coming in from the wilderness, from the wrack of tempest, and the bitter cold, wearied with long marches, footsore or frozen, one looks upon the wooden house as some palace of rest and contentment.

FOR DISCOVERY

1. Assume that you and two of your friends are fur traders who have penetrated into new territory. Discuss the ideal site to build your trading post. What skills would you need to build it?
2. What supplies were stored at the larger forts, or factories?
3. List and explain some of the jobs Company men had to do at the larger forts. If you had the choice, what job would you find most interesting?
4. Assume that you are a clerk who has been given the job of keeping a record of daily events at a fort. Write a page describing the events of a particularly exciting day.

Fort MacPherson, the most northerly post of the Hudson's Bay Company

Transportation

All trade depends on transportation, and nowhere was this more evident than in the fur trade, which spanned an ocean and a continent. Supplies and trade goods had to come from Europe and the furs had to be taken back there. This meant crossing the often turbulent North Atlantic, a hazardous undertaking in the small ocean-going ships of the sixteenth and seventeenth centuries. Because of the constant fear that ships would be lost in storms or in the ice of Davis Strait, York Factory wisely kept a two-year supply of goods and food on hand.

Within North America the expanding fur trade used many different forms of transportation: from the bateaux which plied the treacherous waters of the St. Lawrence, to the birchbark canoes of the western waterways; from the York boats of the northern rivers to the mule trains of the western mountains and the Red River cart brigades of the prairies.

Today, in isolated areas, the canoes, boats and sleds of yesteryear are still used. Elsewhere they have been largely replaced by the train, the truck, the skidoo and the airplane.

Isaac Cowie describes the precautions taken by the Company ship sailing through Davis Strait:

During the passage across Davis Straits, the crew hoisted the crow's nest to the mainmast head, in which to accommodate the lookout when the ship got into the ice. Then a temporary bridge was rigged up, athwart ship, near the mainmast, and projected a few feet outside the bulwarks, to enable the officer of the watch to [guide] the vessel through the ice. Fenders and long spiked poles to protect the vessel's sides and push aside the floes, were also got ready, as well as ice anchors to moor her to the ice, if necessary.

Hudson's Bay Company ship struggling through the ice in Hudson Strait

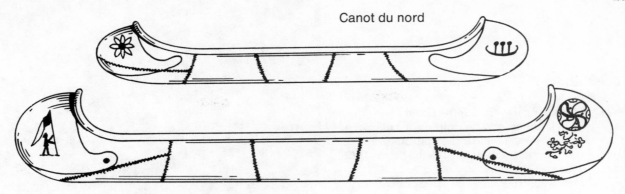

Canot du nord

Canot de maître

Also known as the "Montreal canoe," the *canot de maître* was mainly used on the route from Montreal to Fort William. About 13 m in length, it could carry 4 or 5 tonnes of cargo. The smaller "North canoe" was used mainly on the rivers and smaller lakes north and west of Lake Superior. It varied in size and might be up to 10 m long.

The birchbark canoe was easily damaged, and crews never set out without a supply of bark and gum or pitch for repairs.

The Montreal canoe, or *canot de maître*, carried an incredible amount of goods. Alexander Mackenzie listed the contents of one such canoe which also carried eight or ten men and their baggage:

. . . sixty-five packages of goods, six hundredweight of biscuit, two hundredweight of pork, and three bushels of pease for the men's provision: two oil-cloths to cover the goods, a sail, etc, an axe, a towing-line, a kettle and a sponge to bail out water, with a quantity of gum, bark, and watape [spruce roots] to repair the vessel. An European, on seeing one of these slender vessels thus laden, heaped up, and sunk with her gunwale within six inches of the water, would think his fate inevitable in such a boat when he reflected on the nature of her voyage; but the Canadians are so expert that few accidents happen.

The Portage

A portage (literally "a carrying") occurred whenever the canoe or boat had to be taken from
one river to another, or when rapids or falls forced
the crew to by-pass the hazard. A portage
meant carrying not only the canoe but also all the
cargo. This was conveniently packaged in
pièces, each weighing about 40 kilograms. Every
man was expected to carry two *pièces*. The
first was placed in a leather sling supported by a
"tumpline," or broad strap around the fore-
head. Another *pièce* was then arranged on top of
the first, and when both were in place the
voyageur moved forward slightly bent and at a
shuffling trot. *Canots de maître* were usually
carried upside down by four men, two at the bow
and two at the stern. Two men could manage
the lighter *canot du nord*.

If the portage was fairly long, the
voyageurs would rest periodically. The resting
places were known as *poses*, and the distance
between them varied from 600 to 800 metres
depending on conditions on the trail. In
time many of the longer portages were measured
by the number of *poses* along the trail. The
two longest portages were Grand Portage (14 km)
out of Lake Superior and Methye Portage
(19 km) into the Mackenzie basin.

Portaging remained an important part
of Canadian travel until the building of railways.

Frances Ann Hopkins was the wife of Governor Simpson's secretary. She often accompanied her husband when he travelled west on Hudson's Bay Company business, and she later recorded her experiences in many famous paintings.

Summer insects were a constant annoyance in western Canada. Robert Ballantyne, like many others, complained particularly about the mosquitoes:

As the summer advanced, the heat increased, and the mosquitoes became perfectly insupportable. Nothing can save one from the attacks of these little torments. Almost all other insects went to rest with the sun: sandflies, which bite viciously during the day, went to sleep at night; the large bull-dog, *whose bite is terrible, slumbered in the evening; but the mosquito, whose ceaseless hum dwells for ever in the ear,* never *went to sleep! Day and night, the painful, tender, little pimples on our necks and behind our ears, were being constantly retouched by these villainous flies. It was useless killing thousands of them; millions supplied their place.*

It was not always necessary to portage around an obstacle in a waterway. Sometimes a canoe could be "tracked" or hauled through a rapid, as in this picture. Other times, it could navigate if it were lightened. In such cases the voyageurs carried the freight but not the canoe. This was known as a *décharge* (unloading).

In mountainous areas, goods were often carried by pack horses.

Isaac Cowie describes his experience of a blizzard in the Qu'Appelle valley:

Fortunately, on this occasion we did not have to resort to the usual plan of safety, which consisted in scooping a hole in the snow and spreading robes and blankets under and over one, and lying down to let the snow drift over and protect one from freezing to death from exposure. We had six sleds with large lodge leather wrappers, and these the clever hands of Jerry and his men soon converted to serve the purpose of tent poles and their covering. Arranging the loads of the sleds as a barrier outside of the lodge so formed and taking inside all eatables and the harness to protect them from the dogs, we got inside, and made ourselves secure against the piercing blast, covering the ground with buffalo robes and ourselves with blankets and robes. Then a smoky smudge was started to boil the kettle for tea and to melt snow to drink.

We spent the next twenty-four hours huddled together in this rough refuge from the cold blast of the blizzard, passing the time mostly in sleep, with intervals of eating and smoking, and considered ourselves fortunate in such shelter.

Winter brigade at Lower Fort Garry, 1904. Notice the difference between the freight and passenger sleds.

Red River carts were made entirely of wood. They were drawn either by horses or oxen and could carry over half a tonne of freight. By the 1800s brigades of the sturdy arts were a common sight on prairie trails. Charles Mair describes the noise they made on their ungreased axles:

The creaking of the wheels is indescribable. It is like no sound ever heard in all your life, and makes your blood run cold. To hear a thousand of these wheels all groaning and creaking at one time is a sound never to be forgotten—it is simply hellish.

FOR DISCOVERY

1. Ships sailing from Europe often had to sail against the wind. Explain how this can be done.
2. On a map of the North Atlantic trace the route usually taken by Hudson's Bay Company ships leaving Gravesend for York Factory.
3. The speed of ships is measured in knots. Explain what a "knot" is. If you are in a boat going 50 km/h, what is your speed in knots?
4. Early fur traders used many ways to carry goods—dog sleds, canoes, boats, carts, mules and horses. Explain why. What advantages and disadvantages did each of these methods have?

The sturdy, flat-bottomed York boat was introduced by Governor Simpson to replace the frailer freight canoe on the lakes and bigger rivers.

Voyageurs

The voyageurs are among the best-known figures of Canadian history. The word *voyageur* originally meant simply traveller, but the name was gradually applied to the canoemen who crewed the vessels of the inland fur trade. Though some were Indian and some were Scots from the Orkney Islands, most voyageurs were French Canadian or Métis. They first became important during the days of New France, but reached the height of their fame under the North West Company and later the Hudson's Bay Company. Fur traders, explorers, missionaries, visitors, all depended on the voyageurs as they penetrated to the far North and West. But the voyageurs were more than crewmen. On occasion they became soldiers, and on retirement they became settlers in the little communities which grew up around the old fur-trading forts. They were flamboyant and independent but hardworking and usually dependable. They lived a life unique in Canada—and they lived it to the full.

The Voyageur
The typical voyageur was short but immensely strong. One American traveller commented:

They are short, thick set, and active, and never tire. A Canadian, if born to be a labourer, deems himself to be very unfortunate if he should chance to grow over five feet five, or six inches [about 1.65 m]. ... There is no room for the legs of such people, in these canoes. But if he shall stop growing at about five feet four inches, and be gifted with a good voice, and lungs that never tire, he is considered as having been born under a most favourable star.

After years of paddling, the voyageurs' arms and shoulders developed out of all proportion to the rest of their bodies; and their faces often showed the results of falls, brawls or maulings by wild animals. But all this went unnoticed when they dressed up—and they loved dressing up: a short shirt, a red woollen cap or tuque, deer skin leggings, moccasins, a blue capote, a colourful sash with a beaded bag, and inevitably a pipe in the mouth!

At regular intervals during the day the voyageurs stopped, lit up their pipes and enjoyed a short rest. This routine was so common that distances were often described in "pipes." One pipe was the distance travelled between two smoking breaks, usually seven or eight kilometres.

A lightly laden express canoe running a rapid. Notice that the *avant* (in the bow) and the gouvernail (steersman) are both standing, while the *milieux* (the other crew members) are probably breaking with their paddles.

The Day's Work

The voyageurs certainly worked hard. Speed was essential if they were going to reach their destination and return before their food ran out or the waterways froze.

Their daily routine varied slightly from crew to crew, but usually they were roused well before dawn. They paddled for about six hours before stopping for breakfast at 8 a.m. and then continued until noon. Lunch often consisted of no more than a piece of pemmican hacked off with an axe and chewed while they continued paddling. Throughout the day, however, they enjoyed regular but short breaks during which they stopped paddling for about ten minutes and lit up their pipes. Supper was cooked on the river bank or lake shore about 9 p.m. After a quiet smoke the voyageurs would then settle themselves on the ground with their heads under the upturned canoe for a few hours sleep before work began again the next day.

Few travellers failed to remark on the cheerfulness with which the voyageurs bore their extremely heavy work load. Governor George Simpson, for instance, after describing a typical day on one of his inspection tours, added: "This almost incredible toil the voyageurs bore without a murmur, and generally with such a hilarity of spirit as few other men could sustain for a single forenoon."

The voyageurs were spirited men with a pride all their own. They showed this pride in many ways: in their painted canoes and their speed of paddling, in their dress and songs, in their love of competition, and in their courage and occasional foolhardiness.

The voyageurs chosen to man the canoes of the leading fur traders were doubly proud. Those with experience (*hivernants*) looked down upon the novices (*mangeurs de lard*) while the voyageurs from the distant Athabasca region thought themselves superior to all the others. They often tried to prove this by racing rival canoes, sometimes with near tragic results. One trader recalled:

On the second night of the Contest one of our steersmen fell out of the Stern of his Canoe which being under sail advanced a considerable distance before the people could recover from the confusion that this accident occasioned; in the mean time the poor fellow almost sinking with the weight of his cloathes cried out to 2 Canoes that happened to pass to save his life pour l'amour de dieu; but neither the love of God or of the blessed Virgin, whom he powerfully called to his assistance, had the least influence on his hard hearted Countrymen who paddled along with the greatest unconcern, and he must have certainly perished if his own Canoe had not returned time enough to prevent it.

Voyageurs were famous for their songs, which set the rhythm of their paddling. They sang in French, with the steersman choosing the song and giving the pitch. Some of their songs were based on old tunes their ancestors had brought from France; others they made up themselves about their daily experiences and things they knew about first hand.

Initiation Ceremonies

The voyageurs loved ceremonies. Two of the best known were concerned with the initiation of first-time travellers. John Macdonell describes his initiation in 1793:

I was instituted a North man *by* Batême *performed by sprinkling water in my face with a small cedar Bow dipped in a ditch of water and accepting certain conditions such as not to let any new hand pass by that road without experiencing the same ceremony which stipulates particularly never to kiss a voyageur's wife against her own free will the whole being accompanied by a dozen of Gun shots fired one after another.*

Robert Ballantyne describes another custom that marked a traveller's first trip along a new route:

At sunset we put ashore for the night, on a point covered with a great number of LOPSTICKS. These are tall pine trees, denuded of their lower branches, a small tuft being left at the top. They are generally made to serve as landmarks, and sometimes the voyageurs make them in honour of gentlemen who happen to be travelling for the first time along the route. . . .

The traveller for whom they are made is always expected to acknowledge his sense of the honour conferred upon him by presenting the boat's crew with a pint of grog. . . . He is then considered as having paid for his footing, and may ever afterwards pass scot-free.

Voyageurs as Soldiers

During the war of 1812, a Corps of Canadian Voyageurs was organized with nearly 3000 men. The ill-disciplined and exuberant voyageurs fought bravely in several skirmishes and suffered a few casualties. On the parade ground, however, their appearance and antics clearly exasperated their officers:

They generally came on parade with a pipe in their mouths and their rations of pork and bread stuck on their bayonets. On seeing an officer, whether general, colonel, or subaltern, they took off their hats and made a low bow, with the common saluation of Bon jour, Monsieur le Général, *or* le Colonel. . . . *On parade they talked incessantly, called each other "pork eaters," quarrelled about their rations, wished they were back in Indian country again, &c., and when called to order by their officers and told to hold their tongues, one or more would reply, "Ah, dear captain, let us off as quick as you can; some of us have not yet breakfasted, and it's upwards of an hour since I had a smoke.". . .*

In vain the subaltern winked, in vain the captain threatened, in vain the colonel frowned; neither winks, threats, or frowns, could restrain the vivacious laugh, silence the noisy tongue, or compose the ever changing features into anything like military seriousness.

When a voyageur died on a trip, whether from illness or accident, his colleagues erected a wooden cross to mark his burial place. At some particularly dangerous portages, there might be as many as twenty or thirty such crosses. Other voyageurs passing by would raise their tuques, make the sign of the cross and repeat a short prayer.

FOR DISCOVERY

1. If their life was so hard, why did so many men want to be voyageurs?
2. What jobs today most closely resemble that of the voyageurs?
3. Why did the voyageurs from Athabasca consider themselves superior to all the others?
4. Imagine that you are a *mangeur de lard* on your first trip. Describe in no more than a page the most frightening incident that occurred.
5. The town of Ignace, Ontario, was named in honour of Ignace Mentour, an Indian voyageur. Find three other places named after people associated with the fur trade.

Many a man spent an entire lifetime as a voyageur, and those who survived to old age had few regrets. One retired voyageur summed up the thoughts of many when he said:

Five hundred pounds, twice told, have passed through my hands, although now I have not a spare shirt to my back, nor a penny to buy one. Yet, were I young again, I should glory in commencing the same career again. I would willingly spend another half-century in the same fields of enjoyment. There is no life so happy as a voyageur's life; none so independent; no place where a man enjoys so much variety and freedom as in the Indian country.

Trading for Furs

Trading methods varied from place to place and also changed as time passed. The first contacts took place unexpectedly and with the use of sign language. Later, trading became more regular and more business-like, with the Indians bringing their furs to the great fur fairs of New France.

As traders gradually penetrated into the interior they took along friendly Indians as guides and interpreters and began building small trading posts. Trading was at first quite informal, with trader and supplier haggling over the value of the furs and trade goods.

During the years when the Hudson's Bay Company faced determined competition from the French and later from the Nor'Westers, the Indians had some advantage in the annual barter. When the rival companies merged in 1821, however, the new company had a monopoly and could usually determine the price of its goods in terms of furs. Prices could change if furs were in short supply or in too great abundance.

The Indians quickly became astute traders who refused to accept poor-quality goods in return for their furs.

This painting shows Inuit trading with a Hudson's Bay Company ship in the late 1600s. What would the Inuit be able to trade? What would they want in return?

Rival companies soliciting trade

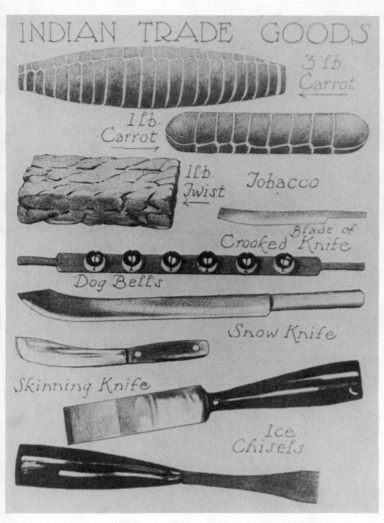

INDIAN TRADE GOODS

3 lb. Carrot

1 lb. Carrot

1 lb. Twist Tobacco

Blade of Crooked Knife

Dog Bells

Snow Knife

Skinning Knife

Ice Chisels

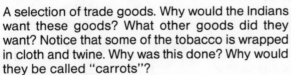

A selection of trade goods. Why would the Indians want these goods? What other goods did they want? Notice that some of the tobacco is wrapped in cloth and twine. Why was this done? Why would they be called "carrots"?

As early as 1613 Champlain commented on the effects of too much competition in the fur trade:

Greediness of gain ... causes the merchants to set out prematurely in order to arrive first in this country. By this means they not only become involved in the ice, but also in their own ruin, for, from trading in a secret manner and offering through rivalry with each other more merchandise than is necessary, they get the worst of the bargain. Thus, while purposing to deceive their associates, they generally deceive themselves.

The Company traders, of course, always wanted furs, but what did the Indians want? At first they were probably quite easily pleased with cheap beads and trinkets. This attitude did not last long, however. They soon became shrewd traders and wanted articles of lasting value: utensils, axes, tools, guns and ammunition. Added to these were a few luxuries such as tobacco, cloth, tea and sugar, and brandy and rum. There even developed a steady demand for quality silver to be used mainly as personal adornment.

At the larger forts, annual trading ceremonies were marked by considerable formality; at the smaller posts trading remained more casual, but the bargaining was just as tough.

Captain James Cook was one of the first Europeans to visit the coast of British Columbia. In his journal he described his first encounters with the Nootka Indians of Vancouver Island:

... A great many canoes, filled with the natives, were about the ships all days; and a trade commenced betwixt us and them, which was carried on with the strictest honesty on both sides. The articles which they offered to sale wing made of the bark of a tree, or some plant like hemp; weapons such as bows, arrows, and spears; fishhooks and instruments of various kinds; wooden visors of many different monstrous figures; a sort of woolen stuff, or blanketing; bags filled with red ochre; pieces of carved work; beads and several other little ornaments of thin brass and iron, shaped like a horse shoe, which they hang on their noses; and several chisels, or pieces of iron, fixed to handles.

Captain Cook's men come ashore to trade

The beaver was so important that it became the medium of exchange in the fur trade. All other pelts were valued in terms of a "made beaver"—a pelt of an adult male beaver in prime condition. In some areas this was called a "castor." In 1854 the Hudson's Bay Company began issuing brass tokens to the value of I, ½, ¼ and ⅛ "made beaver." On the one side is the Company coat of arms; on the other the Company monogram, the initials of the district (East Main) and the value. Notice that the engraver made a mistake and inscribed N. B. instead of M. B.

The North West Company also issued tokens. The head on the token is that of King George IV.

Alexander Mackenzie describes the trade goods provided by the North West Company:

The articles necessary for this trade are coarse woollen cloths of different kinds; milled blankets of different sizes; arms and ammunition; twichester goods; linens and coarse sheetings; thread lines, and twine; common hardware; cutlery and iron-mongery of several descriptions; kettles of brass and copper, and sheet-iron; silk and cotton handkerchiefs, hats, shoes, and hose; calicoes and printed cottons, etc. etc. etc. Spirituous liquors and provisions are purchased in Canada.

Trading ceremony at York Factory

A page from a Hudson's Bay Company Journal showing the standard of trade for 1795.

Robert Ballantyne tells of the possible danger of being too successful!

The number of castors that an Indian makes in a winter hunt varies from fifty to two hundred, according to his perseverance and activity, and the part of the country in which he hunts. The largest amount I ever heard of was made by a man called Piaquata Kiscum, who brought in furs, on one occasion, to the value of two hundred and sixty castors. The poor fellow was soon afterwards poisoned by his relatives, who were jealous of his superior abilities as a hunter.

FOR DISCOVERY

1. Trading at the larger forts took place with great ceremony. Both Indian and trader took part and considered it important. Can you suggest why?
2. Metal kettles were a particularly prized trade item. Why do you think the Indians placed such a high value on them?
3. Many traders married Indian women. How did this help them in their business?
4. If you were an Indian trapper going to barter with the trader at the fort, what are some of the things you could do in order to get higher prices?

Exploration and the Fur Trade

One of the greatest achievements of the fur trade was the exploration of North America. As early as 1670, Jean Talon, the intendant of New France, formally claimed for France all the lands to the west of the Allegheny Mountains in a bid to prevent the expansion of the English colonies on the Atlantic coast. This gesture unleashed an incredible burst of energy as explorers, traders and missionaries from New France penetrated down the Mississippi to the Gulf of Mexico.

This exploration led to domination of the vast area later known as Louisiana, but the region was not good fur country. The Canadian West was far more valuable for the fur trade, and here French exploration was inspired by the great La Vérendrye.

After founding Quebec, Champlain undertook several voyages of exploration. Between 1609 and 1616, he followed the Richelieu River to Lake Champlain, visited the upper Ottawa, travelled as far west as Georgian Bay and then down to the region south of Lake Ontario.

Statue of La Vérendrye in St. Boniface, Manitoba

By 1763 the French had built forts westward to the prairies, while to the north lay the posts of the Hudson's Bay Company. The inland area now covered by the three western provinces and the two territories was largely unknown. Its exploration sprang from the intense rivalry of the two great trading companies and their continuing need to find new sources of furs. Men from both companies set forth and were soon caught up in the excitement of discovery. Three men stand out as the pioneers of this short but great period of exploration: Alexander Mackenzie, Simon Fraser and David Thompson. Mackenzie in 1789 reached the Arctic Ocean and then in 1793 completed his epic journey to the Pacific coast. In 1808 Fraser descended the river that now bears his name; in 1811 Thompson descended the Columbia, only to find the Americans already established at its mouth. The accurate maps Thompson made of the land he travelled served as the basis for all later maps of Western Canada.

Through the explorations of these men, the fur trade did much to shape the extent and boundaries of the future nation of Canada.

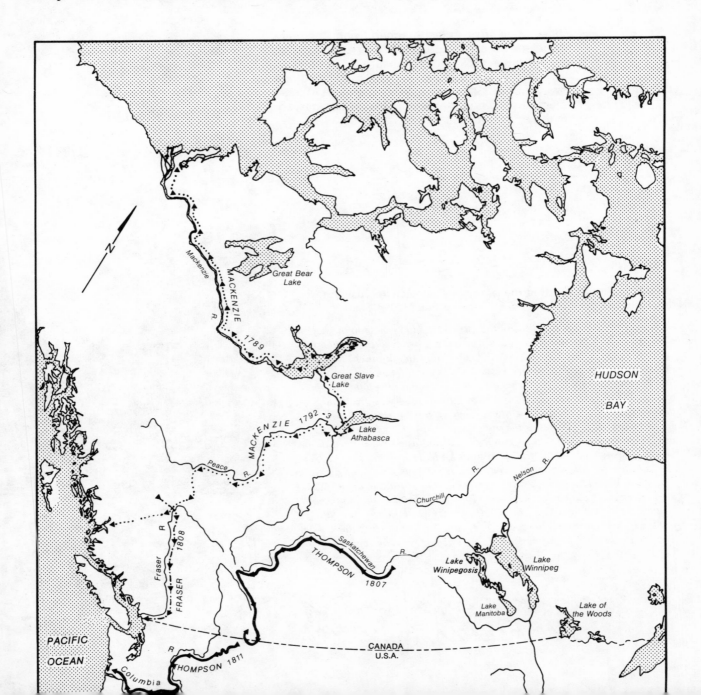

When Mackenzie at last reached Dean Channel, an inlet of the Pacific Ocean, he painted these words on a rock with a mixture of vermillion powder and grease. Rain eventually washed them away, but in 1926 the Historic Sites and Monuments Board had the famous inscription carved in the rock and filled with red cement.

Alexander Mackenzie

Simon Fraser, descending the river which now bears his name, describes the perils of the narrow gorges below Fort George:

As it was impossible to carry the canoes across the land owing to the height of the steep hills, we resolved to venture down. I ordered the five best men of the crews into a canoe lightly loaded; and in a moment it was underway. After passing the first cascade she lost her head and was drawn into an eddy, where she was whirled about, in suspense whether to sink or swim. However, she took a turn from this vortex, flying from one danger to another; but, in spite of every effort, the whirlpool forced her against a low rock. Upon this the men scrambled out, saving their lives; but the greatest difficulty was still ahead. To continue by water would be certain destruction. During this distressing scene we were on shore looking on; but the situation rendered our approach perilous. The bank was high and steep. We had to plunge our daggers into the ground to avoid sliding into the river. We cut steps, fastened a line to the front of the canoe, and hauled it up. Our lives hung upon a thread, as one false step might have hurled us into eternity. However, we cleared the bank before dark. The men had to ascend the immense hills with heavy loads on their backs.

Simon Fraser, descending the Fraser River, 1808

After thirteen years with the Hudson's Bay Company, David Thompson left in 1797 and became a partner in the rival North West Company. He then began fifteen years of exploration and mapping in the Northwest and Pacific coast regions. He vividly recalled in his journal the perils of blizzards on the open prairie:

A gentle south wind arose and kept increasing. By 10 A. M. it was a heavy gale, with high drifts and dark weather.... By noon it was a perfect storm.... Night came on, I could no longer see the compass and had to trust to the wind. The weather became mild with small rain but the storm continued with darkness. Some of the foremost called to lie down where we were, but as it was evident we were ascending a gentle rising ground we continued and soon, thank good Providence, my face struck against some oak saplings and I passed the word that we were in the woods. A fire was quickly made ... but one man and a sled with the dogs were missing. To search for the latter was useless; but how to find the former we were at a loss and remained so for another half an hour, when we thought we heard his voice. The storm was still raging; we extended ourselves within call of each other. The most distant man heard him plainly, went to him, raised him up, and with assistance brought him to the fire, and we all thanked the Almighty for our preservation.

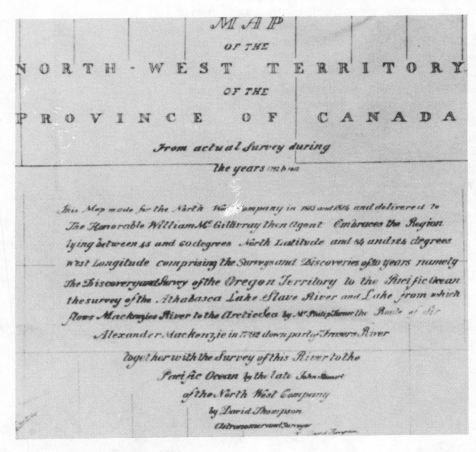

David Thompson was the first white man to travel the full length of the Columbia River. A greater achievement than his actual explorations, however, was his careful surveying of all the land he travelled through. In all, he accurately mapped the main travel routes through more than four million square kilometres of territory.

FOR DISCOVERY

1. What were the main problems faced by explorers in western Canada?
2. If you could have accompanied Alexander Mackenzie on one of his two great explorations, which one would you have chosen? Why?
3. If you were setting off with your crew of voyageurs to explore one of the uncharted rivers of Canada, what would be your greatest fear?

Life in the Fur Trade

Life in the fur trade was often isolated and lonely. Many traders, therefore, sought companionship by marrying Indian women. These women looked after their husbands, taught them to survive in the wilderness and often acted as "go-betweens" in trading with their tribes. They were essential to the fur trade.

As the fur trade grew, conditions changed and became more settled. Company officers brought their Indian or Métis wives to the larger forts where they adopted European customs and raised their children to be educated later in eastern Canada or Britain.

In 1830 Governor Simpson brought his British wife to Red River and other Company officials soon followed his example. Some of these women adjusted well; others did not and tended to look down on the Indian or Métis women they met. For these British wives, life was often lonely but seldom hard. They lived in comfortable homes and had servants to help with their household work and with their children.

The Indian and Métis women had a harder time. They had to look after their families, and this meant cooking, making clothes and often teaching their children. At the larger forts they frequently helped in the farms and gardens; at Red River they joined in the buffalo hunts and made the pemmican on which the fur trade depended.

Children at the trading posts made their own fun but led lonely lives with few friends of their own age. But although life at the fur forts was often hard, a surprising number of men, women and children not only survived but came to enjoy it.

Christmas in Hudson Bay Company territory

Christmas and other holidays were celebrated whenever possible, even at the smallest posts. An entry in the Fort Charles journal as early as 1670 records:

25 being Christmas day wee made merry remembering our Friends in England, having for Liquor Brandy & strong beer & for Food plenty of Partridges & Venison besides what ye shipps provisions afforded.

Christmas ball in Bachelor's Hall

*The Big House at
Lower Fort Garry*

New Year's Day celebrations at Fort Garry
in 1860 were recorded by the first newspaper in
western Canada, the *Nor'Wester*:

*On New Year's Day the post office and stores had closed
for a short time while the postmaster, with a bet
of some pounds on his little Canadian mare Pussy, raced
her on the frozen river against a fast French steed
called Nowhere. The horses were bedecked with rosettes
and ribbons, the enthusiastic crowd milled along
the course and cheered, and the postmaster's little nag,
a stylish beast trained in Detroit, won.*

Robert Ballantyne describes Christmas dinner at York
Factory, 1843:

*We ate it in the winter mess-room, and really (for Hudson's Bay)
this was quite a snug and highly decorated appartment. . . . On the present
grand occasion, [it] was illuminated by an argand lamp, and the
table covered with a snow-white cloth, whereon reposed a platter,
containing a beautiful, fat, plump wild-goose, which had a sort of
come-eat-me-up-quick-else-I'll-melt expression about it that was painfully
delicious. Opposite to this, smoked a huge roast of beef, to procure
which, one of our most useless draught oxen had been sacrificed. This,
with a dozen of white partridges, and a large piece of salt pork,
composed our dinner. But the greatest rarities on the board were two large
decanters of port wine, and two smaller ones of madeira. These were
flanked by tumblers and glasses; and truly, upon the whole, our dinner
made a goodly show.*

*Family sleigh ride
at Red River*

42

James Hargrave's letter to his son Joseph when he was at school in Scotland describes some of the activities of York Factory children:

[Tash] often makes gardens in the ground before her nursery. . . .
Young Rose has had pups and she often has them in the nursery to play
with them. — Two of them are fine large ones and Tash wishes to
have them harnessed to your little carriage which she likes to ride in. . .

Old Mother Morris also brings us very fine Troute from Ten
Shilling Creek where we used to go to catch fish and then get them cooked
on a fire by the side of the stream. . .

Mama and little Mary Jane sometimes take a ride in her Dog Cariole
wrapped up in large Musk ox Robes — with beaver caps and gloves
lined with Ermine. — Little Tash too sometimes goes instead of Mary Jane
and then they take a long ride — out behind the Factory to Nelson
River or down to the Point of Marsh.

Crystal, china and silver-ware much like this was used in the Chief Factor's dining room at York Factory. Why, do you think, was such elaborate tableware brought out to wilderness posts?

The Chief Factors and traders in charge of the larger forts usually enjoyed good food. Dr. Helmeken visited York Factory and dined with Chief Factor James Hargrave and his wife, Letitia:

Hargrave descanted on the beauties of "white fish" of
which some small ones were on the table. . . .
However, ducks came on — and asked whether I would
take duck or goose — duck — so a whole one was
put on my plate! Not a very large one to be sure, but I
did not know how to begin eating it, but before I
had begun, my neighbour had sent for another.

Ice fishing and other winter activities at the junction of the Red and Assiniboine Rivers

Cross-writing was commonly used to save space in letters and cut down the cost of postage.

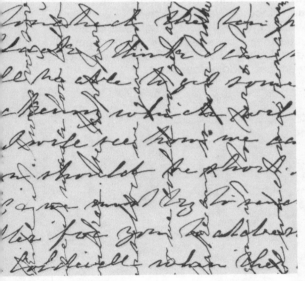

Goose hunting at Point of Marsh, near York Factory

Henry Martin Robinson, an American traveller and writer, describes how the young employees of the larger posts fill their leisure hours:

In the summer season, recourse is had to athletic exercises during the long twilights — rowing upon the rivers, pitching quoits, equestrian excursions....

[In winter] conversation and the peaceful pipe occupy a prominent position in the passage of time. Games, too, are in great demand, and every apartment possesses its well-thumbed pack of cards, its rude cribbage-board, and sets of wooden dominoes. Reading men find abundant leisure to pursue their favorite occupation during the long winter evenings....

Parties not studiously inclined often pass their spare hours in exercising their skill upon one of the musical instruments. Of these the violin, on account probably of its portable nature, is most ordinarily selected.... Under the inspiration of this instrument, it is scarcely to be wondered at that the few holidays of the year, and frequently the long evenings also, should be enlivened with dances.... It is in the enjoyment of this pastime that the wearied clerk finds his chief delight; and he jigs and reels the hours away to the measures of monotonous and oft-repeated tunes.

FOR DISCOVERY

1. What are some of the things you would like or dislike about living at a fur fort?
2. Are there any jobs today that would be as lonely as being a fur trader in the early 1800s?
3. Imagine that you are a twelve year old living at York Factory with your family. Write to a favourite aunt in Scotland asking her to send you a parcel in the next Company ship. What would you ask her to send?
4. Many traders had Métis wives. Some of these women, like Amelia Douglas, wife of Sir James Douglas, played a prominent role in society. Some European wives like Letitia Hargrave, however, found it difficult to adjust to life in an isolated fur fort. Read about one of these women and write a brief biography.

From Fur to Garment

To change the fur of a living animal into a fashionable coat is a complicated process. Once the animal is killed, the skin or pelt is removed. There are two ways of doing this: *cased* and *open*. Cased pelts are removed from the animal by slitting the pelt across the rump and pulling it over the animal's head in the way that we peel off a pullover. All pelts except beaver, bear and seal are prepared in this way. Open pelts are removed by slitting the fur on the underside of the animal and peeling back the pelt one side at a time.

When a cased pelt has been taken from the carcass it, has first to be cooled until the fat has hardened. It is then placed on a fleshing board, and the fat is gently scraped off, care being taken not to cut the skin. Every scrap of fat has to be removed or the fur will spoil. After stretching, the pelt is dried by hanging for up to sixty hours in a room temperature of about 15°••C. Pelts are then ready for shipping.

In the case of open pelts, all excess grease is carefully removed as the pelt is being taken from the carcass. The pelt is then thoroughly cleaned in lukewarm water, stretched on a board and removed when dry. After brushing, it is ready for shipment to a buyer.

The first public auction of Hudson's Bay Company furs was held in 1672 in the hall of Garraway's Inn, a famous London coffee house. Both the Prince of Wales and the Duke of York were among the spectators. A lighted candle on the auctioneer's desk was the most common method of limiting bids at fur auctions: when the flame went out, bidding ceased.

Sorting furs at The Pas, Manitoba, 1915

Winnipeg policeman in buffalo coat, 1930s

This Indian woman is stretching a beaver skin on a frame in order to scrape it.

Furs eventually reach an auction house where they are graded, sorted, classified and offered for sale. The main Canadian fur auctions are held at Winnipeg, Montreal and North Bay, Ontario.

But there is still much to do before the fur becomes a garment. Some pelts are dyed, and most are cleaned in revolving drums containing sawdust to absorb excess moisture. A final rubbing brings out the lustre. The fur is then ready for the experts who match them for quality and appearance, the designers who create the patterns, and the cutters and nailers who shape the fur to the design. Sleeves, pockets, collars and cuffs are added, the lining is sewn in, and the coat is complete.

FOR DISCOVERY

1. To what extent have furs been used in clothing for men?
2. Today there are many kinds of material that are warmer and lighter than fur. What are some of these? Why are furs still in great demand?

Effects of the Fur Trade

Over a period of four hundred years the fur trade has influenced the building of Canada. Demand for furs led first to French settlement and then to British. Settlement and intermarriage with native Indians produced a new race, the proud Métis who first won fame as voyageurs.

Competition for furs led ultimately to the exploration of the Northwest and its opening to agricultural and industrial settlement. By this time, the native peoples had become dependent on the tools, weapons and other goods supplied by the fur traders. Gradually they lost many of their ancestral skills. Forced onto reserves, the Indians also lost much of their pride as a people. Resentment, frustration and bitterness grew; and these feelings are still common today. Yet an increasing number of Canadian native people—Indian, Métis and Inuit—are now rediscovering a sense of pride and determination that will make them citizens of Canada in the fullest sense.

Native farmer

Native populations declined significantly after the arrival of the fur traders. The major cause was epidemic diseases, introduced by the Europeans, to which the native people had no immunity. This trend eventually reversed itself, but living conditions for native people remained very poor. In the early years of this century many still died from infectious diseases. Chief George Baker recalls one outbreak of smallpox:

When I was very young many of my people in Bloodvein died from smallpox. I remember quite well walking to a neighbour's log cabin. It was one of the few cabins around; most people, including ourselves, lived in wigwams. They had a large family. As I opened the door to enter I will never forget the odour. It smelled awful. I walked inside and everyone was still in bed. This was unusual because every other time I went there, the family would all be up. I didn't stay long. I ran back and told grandma. She scolded me and said, "cou-cou-cou," which means "lost" or "dead." The whole family had died....

During the sickness no doctor came. It wasn't until only a few cases were left that the doctor and two policemen arrived.

Indian children at residential school, 1915

The spread of settlement and the extension of the national boundaries to the Arctic greatly affected the Inuit people. They were expected to adopt a European way of life, and this often meant education away from home. Alice French, an Inuit, was born in 1930 on Baillie Island in the Northwest Territories. She went to boarding school at Aklavik at the age of seven.

My teacher's name was Miss A. Farrow and after Christmas her job was much easier for we were all able to speak fairly well in English. I was luckier than some of my girl friends, because I had learned English from my father. We had not been allowed to speak our native tongue since coming to school and it was hard on some of my friends. If we were caught speaking in Eskimo we were punished. This was a frustrating but effective system....

Despite being a hero, like many Indians Tommy Prince met prejudice when he returned home after the Korean war:

Tom's first job was as a sweeper and cleaner, on the night shift, at a large ice cream manufacturing plant in Winnipeg. He proved to be a good steady worker, but some men refused to work with him because he was Indian. . . . The manager of the plant tried hard to get men who would work with an Indian and often would enourage Tom to "stick it out." Finally, Tom could stand the humiliation no longer, and, despite the pleas of the manager, quit the job. It was a bitter lesson to learn, and it changed his personality.

Chief Dan George recalls how he dealt with ignorance about Indians on one occasion when he was on a plane travelling to Ottawa:

There was this man, walkin' up and down, looking at me. He looked and looked. I guess he'd never seen a real live Indian before. He went back and forth a long time; then he came over and said very slowly, "You. You been long away from reservation?" I just looked straight ahead and said, "Yes. Me paddle many moons in my canoe."

Monument to Louis Riel at Manitoba Legislative Building

FOR DISCOVERY

1. Explain the meaning of the terms *Métis* and *Inuit*.
2. If there are Indians living in your province, try to find out how many there are, where they live, what kinds of jobs they do and what languages they speak.
3. Many Métis played important roles in the history of western Canada. The most famous is probably Louis Riel. Read more about him and write a short biography.
4. The Indians and the Inuit feel that many modern projects such as pipelines and hydro-generating stations will destroy their traditional way of life. Why are these projects seen as threats? Should they be stopped?

Inuit children at school in 1980s

48

Selected Further Reading

Andrews, R.J. *The Fur Fort*. Toronto: Ginn and Company, 1970. A well-illustrated account of the role of the forts in the fur trade, with details of construction, location and of the trading ceremonies.

_____. *The Beaver*. Winnipeg: Hudson's Bay House. A quarterly magazine about the part of Canada that was once controlled by the Hudson's Bay Company.

Campbell, Marjorie Wilkins. *The Fur Trade*. (Jackdaw Kit C5). Toronto: Clarke, Irwin, 1971. An interesting kit containing extensive notes, pictures and facsimiles of documents.

_____. *The Nor'Westers*. Toronto: Macmillan, 1973. A detailed account of the North West Company from its beginnings until it merged with the Hudson's Bay Company in 1821.

Healy, W.J. *Women of Red River*. Winnipeg: Peguis, 1967. Recollections, first published in 1923, of the women of the Red River Settlement.

The Manitoba Trappers' Guide. Winnipeg: Department of Mines, Natural Resources and Environment, 1979. Details of trapping methods and regulations.

Morse, Eric W. *Fur Trade Canoe Routes of CanadaThen and Now*. Toronto: University of Toronto Press, 1979. A thorough account of the canoe routes and the problems they presented, based on first-hand experience.

Neering, Rosemary. *Fur Trade*. Toronto: Fitzhenry & Whiteside, 1974. A straight-forward account of the fur trade for younger readers.

Wilson, Clifford. *Adventurers from the Bay*. Toronto: Macmillan, 1962. The story of the men of the Hudson's Bay Company and their work in what is now western Canada.

Wilson, Keith. *Fur Trade in Canada*. Toronto: Grolier, 1980. The history of the fur trade and the role it played in the exploration and development of Canada.

_____. *George Simpson and the Hudson's Bay Company*. Agincourt: Book Society of Canada, 1977. The colourful career of Simpson is set in the context of the rise and gradual decline of the fur trade.

_____. *The Red River Settlement*. Toronto: Grolier, 1983. A lively description of life at Red River from the arrival of the Selkirk settlers to the formation of the province of Manitoba.

Illustration Credits

Abbreviations: T—top; M—middle; B—bottom; L—left; R—right

Cover: Manitoba Archives (MA); p. 2 T: Hudson's Bay Company (HBC); B: The National Gallery, London; p. 4: Ontario Ministry of Natural Resources (OMNR); p. 5 T & B: OMNR; M: MA; p. 6 T: Greenpeace Foundation; B: OMNR; p. 7: OMNR; p. 8: Public Archives of Canada (PAC) C33615; p. 9 T: PAC C70289; B: Royal Ontario Museum (ROM); p. 10 T: Woodstream Corporation; B: PAC C13471; p. 11: MA; p. 12: PAC C69731; p. 13 T: PAC C12005; B: HBC; p. 14 T: PAC C164; M: Ontario Ministry of Industry and Tourism (OMIT); B: HBC; p. 15: HBC; p. 16: PAC C7348; p. 17 T: PAC C82981; B: PAC A1712; p. 18 T: HBC; B: OMIT; p. 19 T: MR & BR: OMIT; ML & BL: Media Services, Manitoba Department of Education (MDE); p. 20 T: HBC; B: HBC; B: MA; p. 21 T: PAC; B: Alberta Archives; p. 22: MDE; p. 23 M: MDE; B: PAC C2772; p. 24 T: PAC C73678; M: MA; B: PAC C2771; p. 25 T: Glenbow Alberta Institute (GA); B: ROM; p. 26 T: HBC; B: MA; p. 27 T: MA; B: GA; p. 29 2T: MDE; B: MA; p. 30 T: MDE; B: Manitoba Historical Society; p. 31: PAC C2336; p. 32 L: PAC C73431; R: HBC; p. 33 L: PAC; R: PAC C16859; p. 34 T: PAC C6641; M & B: HBC; p. 35L: MA; R: HBC; p. 36 L: PAC C13320; R: MA; p. 38 T & M: Provincial Archives of British Columbia; B: PAC C71270; p. 39: MDE; p. 40L: MDE; R: HBC; p. 41 TL: MA; TR: PAC C73598; B: C1941; p. 42 M: PAC C25169; B: PAC C1932; p. 43: MA; p. 44: HBC; p. 45 TR & ML: MA; MR: PAC; B: HBC; p. 46: MA; p. 47 T: MA; M: MDE; BL: Manitoba Government Travel; BR: Department of Indian Affairs and Northern Devlopment.